VOLUME

3

FABLES
& THEIR MORALS

THE LION AND THE MOUSE
to
THE REDBREAST AND THE SPARROW

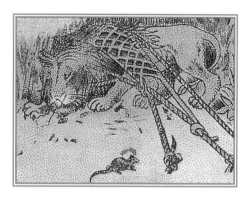

by

Bruce and Becky Durost Fish

Chelsea House Publishers
Philadelphia

CHELSEA HOUSE PUBLISHERS

Editor in Chief Stephen Reginald
Managing Editor James D. Gallagher
Production Manager Pamela Loos
Art Director Sara Davis
Picture Editor Judy Hasday
Senior Production Editor Lisa Chippendale
Designers Takeshi Takahashi, Keith Trego

First Printing

1 3 5 7 9 8 6 4 2

Library of Congress Cataloging-in-Publication Data

Fish, Bruce.
Fables and their morals / by Bruce and Becky Durost Fish.
    p. cm.
Includes bibliographical references and index.
Summary: Illustrated retelling of one hundred classic fables
from around the world.

ISBN 0-7910-5210-9 (set), 0-7910-5211-7 (vol. 1),
0-7910-5212-5 (vol. 2), 0-7910-5213-3 (vol. 3),
0-7910-5214-1 (vol. 4)
1. Fables. 2. Tales. [1. Fables. 2. Folklore.] I. Fish, Becky
Durost. II. Title.
PZ8.2.F54Fab 1999   98–36355
398.2—dc21   CIP
                                                        AC

CONTENTS

INTRODUCTION

Fables are stories that feature animals with human characteristics. The animals' experiences teach us lessons about life and the way people behave. The word *fable* comes from the Latin word *fabula*, which means "a telling." While the stories usually end with a moral that summarizes what the story is teaching, the emphasis is on the story itself.

Fables are one of the oldest forms of stories. Before it was easy to write things down, they were passed on orally. Parents or wise people in a village would tell the stories to the children, who would grow up and pass the stories on to their children. Originally fables were told as poems because it is easier to memorize words that rhyme and have rhythm than it is to remember prose.

One of the most famous fable writers was Aesop. Many people think he lived in or near Greece during the sixth century B.C. and created about 200 fables. As far as we know, Aesop never wrote down his fables. The first person known to have put Aesop's fables into a collection was Demetrius of Phaleron, who lived in the fourth century B.C.

Aesop's fables have remained popular for 2,600 years, making him one of the most successful figures in the history of literature. His stories spread throughout Greece and Rome. When the Roman Empire expanded as far as Britain, soldiers carried Aesop's stories with them all across what is now Europe. His stories even traveled to Japan. When Jesuit missionaries arrived in Japan during the 16th century, they taught Aesop's fables to the Japanese.

But Aesop's stories are not the only fables we know of from ancient times. Many scholars believe that fables in India date back to the fifth century B.C. They were first used to instruct followers of the Buddha about his teachings. Many of these early stories are called *Jakatas*. They are birth stories about the Buddha and tell some of his experiences when incarnated as different animals, that is, when he was born as various animals. These stories include morals.

Another important group of fables from India is called the *Pancatantra*. The *Pancatantra* was originally written in Sanskrit. The oldest copy of it available is an Arabic translation from the eighth century called the *Kalilah wa Dimnah*. The stories feature two jackals who counsel a lion king. The tales teach political wisdom and cunning. They were translated into many languages, and in the 13th century a Latin version reached Europe.

For centuries, China did not have fables because traditional Chinese thought did not accept the idea of animals thinking and behaving like humans. The Chinese preferred stories based on actual events. But between the fourth and sixth centuries, trade with India made Chinese Buddhists familiar with the Indian fables that helped explain Buddhist teachings. Chinese Buddhists adapted these fables and collected them in the book *Po-Yü ching*.

Japan also has a tradition of fables. Well before Aesop's fables reached Japan, the Japanese had official histories from the first and eighth centuries that featured stories about small, intelligent animals getting the better of big, stupid creatures.

Bernard Binlin Dadié, a 20th-century writer from the Ivory Coast, published several books of African fables and folktales that he collected from that continent's oral traditions. As in other regions of the world, African fables feature animals with human characteristics.

Because of the continuing popularity of fables, many authors have written their own collections. Some fables became quite long. These expanded stories are called *beast epics*. The most famous example of a beast epic is *Roman de*

Renart, written in the 12th century. It contains related stories about Renart the Fox, who represents a cunning man. But most fables are much shorter and in the style of Aesop.

The 12th century also produced a book of short fables by Marie de France, a French poet. Her book was called *Ysopets* and was very popular.

Another French poet, Jean de La Fontaine, published a 12-book collection of fables between 1668 and 1693. Titled *Fables,* these stories are among the greatest masterpieces of French literature. Some experts consider La Fontaine's fables to be the best ever written.

In the late 19th century, publishers began producing many more children's books. Because of this, more authors began using fables in their work. Lewis Carroll (whose real name was Charles Dodgson) released *Alice's Adventures in Wonderland* in 1865. Its animal characters such as the rabbit and the walrus have human qualities. Beatrix Potter self-published *The Tale of Peter Rabbit* in 1900. It was picked up by Frederick Warne and Company in 1902, and the collection of stories about Peter, his family, and Farmer McGregor became one of the best-selling children's books of all time.

Kenneth Grahame's *The Wind in the Willows* with its animal characters Mole, Rat, Badger, and Toad was published in 1908. And Christopher Robin's toy animal friends in *Winnie-the-Pooh* (1926) and *The House at Pooh Corner* (1928), by A. A. Milne, act like human beings and teach lessons about life.

In the 20th century, the use of fable took a darker turn with the publication in 1945 of George Orwell's *Animal Farm.* With the famous line "All animals are equal, but some animals are more equal than others," Orwell's story of animals in a farmyard pilloried Josef Stalin and his oppressive government in the U.S.S.R.

Watership Down, by Richard Adams, and *The Redwall Books,* by Brian Jacques, also draw on the fable tradition. Many science fiction fantasy books, such as J.R.R. Tolkien's

The Hobbit and *The Lord of the Rings* trilogy, use elements of the fable to give a greater sense of reality to the imaginary worlds where they take place.

As new means of storytelling have emerged, the fable has continued to be used effectively. Elements of the fable can be found in comic strips such as *Peanuts,* by Charles Schulz; *The Far Side,* by Gary Larson; and *Shoe,* by Jeff MacNelly. Movies such as *Babe* and *The Lion King* are fables presented through film.

Considering that fables have remained popular for thousands of years, it may only be a matter of time before they are adapted to computer games, virtual reality programs, and other creative avenues yet to be developed.

AESOP

Exactly who Aesop was remains a mystery. Some people think he never existed. They say that Aesop is a legendary figure who was invented to give a name to the anonymous creators of the roughly 200 fables that are attributed to him.

But from ancient times, people have told stories about Aesop and his life. Herodotus, a Greek historian who lived in the fifth century B.C., wrote that Aesop was a slave who lived in the sixth century B.C. Most other stories about Aesop agree that he was a sixth-century slave. One story says that his master Jadmon was so impressed with Aesop's wisdom that he freed the slave.

Stories differ about where Aesop was from. Some say that he was from Thrace, others that he was from Phrygia. An Egyptian biography written in the first century places Aesop as a slave on the island of Samos. Plutarch, a first-century Greek biographer, wrote that Aesop was an adviser to Croesus, the king of Lydia. While the places differ, they all are in or near what is now Greece and Turkey.

After Aesop was freed from slavery, stories tell of him traveling throughout the ancient world, advising rulers and telling stories to both teach and entertain. Some accounts say that Aesop went to the ancient kingdom of Babylon (modern Iran) and became a riddle solver for King Lycurgus.

Another story tells of Aesop visiting Athens and the court of its ruler Peisistratus. He convinced the citizens of Athens to keep Peisistratus as ruler by telling them the fable "The Frogs Who Wanted a King" (see volume 2 of this series).

A 14th-century monk named Maximus Planudes who

admired Aesop's fables described him as an ugly deformed dwarf. Earlier biographers don't mention Aesop's appearance. Many people think that if Aesop were so disfigured, people living closer to his time would have mentioned it.

Herodotus wrote that Aesop died in the Greek city of Delphi, an important religious center. Apparently the citizens became angry with Aesop and threw him off a cliff, but there are several differing accounts of what provoked their attack.

In one story, Croesus, the king of Lydia, sent Aesop as an ambassador to Delphi with a large sum of gold to distribute among the citizens. When Aesop arrived, he was so appalled by the citizens' greed that he refused to give them the gold. Instead he sent the money back to Croesus.

Another writer claims that the people of Delphi were offended by the sarcastic tone of Aesop's fables. Still others suggest that Aesop died as a punishment for embezzling money from Croesus or for stealing a silver cup.

Whatever the truth may be about Aesop's life and death, his stories continue to entertain and enlighten new generations of readers.

THE LION AND
THE MOUSE

In the high grass, at the base of a large tree, a lion lay fast asleep in the shade. A small gray mousewife did not see him until she darted across his nose.

With a snort, the lion woke up and sent the mouse tumbling to the ground. As she lay stunned, the lion trapped her under one huge paw.

"What have we here," he said, "an afternoon snack?"

"It would not be worth your trouble to eat one so small as me," said the mouse, more irritated than afraid. "If you let me go, I promise to repay your kindness."

The lion roared with laughter. "What could one so small as you possibly do for me? I am the king of the beasts."

"Even kings need help sometimes," insisted the mouse.

The lion grew thoughtful. "I will release you because of your courage, but I doubt that I will ever need your help."

With that, he lifted his paw. The mouse gave him a respectful bow and ran off into the forest.

Weeks later as she was gathering food, the mouse found the lion thrashing wildly on the ground, trying to escape from a heavy net.

"Lie still, and I can help you," the mouse commanded. She began to gnaw on the ropes, and soon the lion was free.

"I am deeply in your debt," said the lion in a quiet voice. "Come ride on my back and tell me what I can do for your family."

Moral: Acts of kindness are often rewarded in unexpected ways.

THE MAN AND
THE LION

man and a lion became close friends after each saved the other's life. One day they were walking together through the oldest part of a large, dark forest.

At the top of a small hill, they found a round clearing covered with grey paving stones. In its center stood a 20-foot-tall marble statue of a man wrestling with a lion. An inscription on its base read: "Hercules slays the Nemean lion."

"Nonsense," growled the lion. "No human could kill one of my kind with his bare hands."

"I'm afraid you're wrong, my friend," replied the man. "Hercules was a great hero to both the Romans and the Greeks. The Greeks called him Heracles. Their ancient myths say that as a baby, he strangled two serpents who crawled into his crib, sent by the jealous queen of the gods. The myths say he was one of the strongest men who ever lived".

"But this statue is all wrong," insisted the lion. "The man is too large, and the lion is too small. No man has muscles that big. Look at the way he is holding the lion, with his arm around its neck, and trying to choke it from behind. Any fit and healthy lion could break that hold in a moment and tear the fool into bloody bits.

"Obviously a man made that statue," continued the lion. "If a lion had carved it, the man would be the vanquished, not the victor."

Moral: Those who tell the stories cast themselves in the role of the hero.

THE MAN, HIS SON, AND HIS DONKEY

A farmer and his son set out with their donkey for a nearby village. Two travelers on fine horses soon passed them.

"All farmers are fools," said one loudly to the other. "Those two both walk when one could be riding."

At once the farmer told his son to get up on the donkey.

A little later, they passed a very proper woman on the road. She shouted at the boy, "Young man, have you no manners? Get down this instant and let your father ride!"

"Perhaps it would be best," said the father.

Near the village, two young women met them. "Look at that lazy old man," remarked one. "He rides while his son walks."

The father immediately asked his son to ride behind him.

Just outside the village, some merchants were waiting to cross a stone bridge over a swift river.

"Such cruelty," exclaimed a merchant. "Those farmers

look more able to carry the donkey than he does to carry them."

The son jumped off the donkey. "We have never abused our animals," he shouted in disgust.

The father got down and stood beside him. "Lend us a pole from your wagon and some rope," he said angrily, "and we'll prove it to you."

They tied the donkey's feet together and carried him, suspended from the pole. As they slowly crossed the bridge, the donkey began to bray and kick. The pole broke, and the helpless animal tumbled over the edge of the bridge and down into the cold, swirling water.

Moral: Only fools try to please everyone around them.

THE MASTIFF AND
THE GOOSE

 young goose grew up around a quiet pond in the center of a farmer's field. The pond was always filled with well water, even during the hottest part of the summer. Every animal around used the pond for drinking, bathing, and playing. The goose got along with all of them until her first chicks were born. Then everything changed.

The young goose wanted to make sure her chicks were always safe. The first sign of trouble came when she began shooing the other animals away from the grassy end of the pond where she lived.

As the chicks grew and began to explore more of the pond, their mother saw danger everywhere. First she threatened the small birds and field mice, and soon she honked and snapped at even the large animals.

When she attacked the dairy cows and scared them so

badly they gave only half as much milk as usual, the farmer began to worry.

Early one morning, he brought his mastiff to the pond. He told the huge golden watchdog to sniff around for the fox or other wild animal that was frightening his cows. When the mastiff stopped to drink from the pond, the goose attacked him.

The mastiff slapped her aside with one paw and then bit her so hard that she was never able to fly again. As the bloodied goose hobbled away, the dog quietly drank his fill.

Forever after, the goose was afraid to leave the tall grass at the end of the pond.

Moral: Those who misuse their authority soon lose it.

MERCURY AND THE WOODSMAN

 greedy and corrupt nobleman over the course of several years finally cheated an honest and hardworking woodsman out of nearly everything he owned.

One day, a few months later, the woodsman was felling trees near a small lake. He grew tired and sweaty as he swung his axe in the hot sun. Suddenly, the axe slipped out of his hands and flew over a rocky ledge into deep water. He shouted in despair, for it was his last good axe.

The god Mercury saw his distress and dove into the dark water. He came up holding an axe of pure gold.

"Is this your axe?" he asked.

The woodsman replied, "That is a beautiful axe, but it is not mine."

Mercury dove again and returned with a hardened steel axe that looked brand new.

"I appreciate your honesty," he said. "Your axe has been

healed of all wear and will never need sharpening again. The golden axe I give you as a gift, to restore prosperity to your family."

When the corrupt nobleman heard about the golden axe, he rode to the lake and tossed in an old, dull axe.

Once again Mercury appeared with a golden axe from the lake. The nobleman claimed it as his own.

"Then take what is yours," said Mercury.

As the nobleman grasped the axe, it turned to lead.

"This is the reward for your greed and dishonesty," said Mercury sternly.

When the nobleman returned home, all his possessions had turned to lead.

Moral: Honesty is the best policy.

THE MICE IN
COUNCIL

he mice in an old manor house had lived for many years in peace with their human and animal neighbors. One day, the owner of the house brought a new cat home for his young daughter. This cat had no respect for the traditional order of things and chased the mice every time they crept out of their hole.

The mice called an emergency meeting of their ruling council to deal with this new threat. They discussed tactics and plotted strategies long into the night.

One suggested that they replace the cheese in the mouse-traps that the cook always put out for them (and in which he never caught anything) with food from the cat's dish.

Another suggested putting a mixture of honey and arsenic near some of their holes in the hope that the new cat would walk through it and then try to clean his paws, thus bringing about his death.

Finally they arrived at a plan that seemed both fair and effective. They would attach a small brass bell around the cat's neck while he was asleep. That way they would always hear him coming and could keep a safe distance away.

They were all congratulating themselves on the boldness and wisdom of this plan when an old and much respected mouse twitched his whiskers to speak.

"I have only one question," he said in his wise old voice. "Which of you heroes is going to put that bell around the cat's neck?"

Moral: There is a world of difference between bold talk and bold deeds.

THE MISCHIEVOUS DOG

A brown, floppy-eared hound dog liked nothing better than to bite people and animals on the back of the leg. He was always careful not to draw blood, but no one liked his behavior, which made him the talk of the small town where he lived.

He bit the mailman and the milkman and the pastor of the local church. He bit other dogs and cats and horses and cows. Anything with legs was fair game to him.

His owner, who was a respected medical doctor, was forever apologizing for the mischievous dog and looking for ways to stop his outrageous behavior.

First he tried a muzzle, the most obvious solution, but the dog couldn't breathe properly while wearing it.

Next he tried a long leash made from strong rope. This worked until his dog discovered a new game. He called it "Wrap the Leash Around Every Leg I See." He enjoyed wrapping legs almost as much as he liked biting them.

Finally the doctor attached a cowbell around the dog's neck. Since everyone could hear the animal coming, his sneak attacks became impossible.

The hound dog was very proud of his bell. He thought it was a reward for clever behavior. One day he was bragging about it to an Irish wolfhound, one of the few creatures he had never tried to bite.

"This is no award for good behavior," his friend pointed out. "It's a sign of your foolishness."

Moral: Those who are famous are not always successful.

THE MISER

A miser lived a very penny-pinching existence in a big old house that he had inherited from his grandparents. He had been kind and generous in his youth, but as he grew older he became obsessed with protecting his wealth.

The house was deteriorating because he refused to pay for necessary repairs and maintenance. Half the lamps didn't have wicks. The old man kept replacing bad wicks with good ones from lamps in other parts of the house. He didn't want to spend money on new wicks that he might never use.

He hid much of his wealth in a steel strongbox buried in the backyard near an old oak tree. Every week the miser checked to make sure everything was safe.

A gardener who worked next door observed this ritual and made plans to steal the miser's wealth. On the next

moonless night, the gardener crept into the backyard, pried open the box, and removed all its contents.

A few days later, the miser discovered his loss. He wailed loudly and beat his fists against the old oak tree until they were bloody.

A neighbor heard the cries and rushed over to help.

After the miser explained his loss, the neighbor remarked, "Why are you so upset to lose things you never intended to use? Fill the strongbox with old newspapers and rocks. You can still come out here each week and pretend to admire your wealth. Nothing about your life needs to change."

Moral: Even in the midst of wealth, misers remain poor.

The Nightingale
and the Bat

ne warm spring evening a nightingale sang. Her cage hung on the porch of an old white house on a tree-lined street. As she looked out through the bars, she remembered happier days when she had been free.

A friendly bat flitted across the lawn just beyond the porch. The nightingale watched him twisting and diving in the night air between the flowering bushes close to the house and the trees along the street.

When the bat grew tired of picking insects out of the air, he turned toward the porch. He landed on top of the nightingale's cage, then folded his wings and hung upside down from the wire frame. His beady black eyes reflected the light from the house.

In a squeaky voice he asked, "Why is it that you only sing at night?"

"Two years ago, I was flying among the beautiful trees of

an ancient forest when I was caught in a fowler's net," said the nightingale. "From that day to this I have lived in cages. I was caught because I revealed my presence in the forest by singing during the day. Now, I only sing at night to remind myself of my foolishness and to warn other birds who still are free."

"But no one except you knows why you sing only at night. Why not give yourself the pleasure of singing during the day?" replied the bat. "As for your fate, how can singing in the daytime make anything worse, since you are already caged?"

Moral: A foolish reason for doing something is worse than no reason at all.

The Nurse and the Wolf

A hungry wolf spent the day hunting for food in the woods and meadows surrounding a small town. Not even a mouse did he find. As the sun set, he made his way into the town itself, keeping to the back alleys and vacant lots. He hoped to capture some chickens or even a house cat to fill his empty stomach.

He slipped into the back garden of a house with a large chicken coop. He could smell the chickens inside but could find no way to get at them. While he stood in the backyard, he heard a child crying inside the house.

A woman was scolding the child. "Keep your hands away from that or I will throw you outside for the wolves to eat!"

"Now here is something worth waiting for," thought the wolf. "Human children almost never obey the first time they are warned."

He moved like a shadow across the garden, covering half

the distance to the back of the house, where he hid behind
the tool shed.

"I want it!" wailed the child.

The nurse raised her voice. "All right, out you go!"

Slowly the wolf crept toward the back door.

"Noooo!" cried the child. "I'm sorry. Please don't let the
wolves eat me!"

"I would never really do that," replied the woman, "But I
had to say something so you would stop trying to open the
oven door and eat those hot cookies. I was afraid you would
be burned."

Moral: Never trust words spoken in desperate circumstances.

THE OAK AND
THE WILLOW

giant oak tree stood beside a forest stream, where many willow bushes grew along the banks. One day, the eastern sky grew dark with clouds boiling up over the sea many miles away.

Through its layers of gnarled bark, the old oak felt the air pressure begin to drop. He smelled salt in the air. As the billowing clouds grew on the horizon, he measured their size, shape, and motion against a thousand memories of other storms from hundreds of years in the past.

"This will be a great storm, greater than most of you children have ever seen," he warned the plants and animals in the surrounding woods. "We must summon all our strength and courage to face it."

The willows near the stream swayed in the rising winds. "Do not worry about us," they whispered. "For generations we have bent before storms, while you have faced them

upright. Each time we worry as you creak and groan in the wind and wonder when your great strength will fail you."

"Children," replied the oak, "My strength will never fail. As I have stood for centuries, so I will always stand."

That night the wind howled, carrying torrents of rain in horizontal sheets. Lightning crackled for hours, and thunder rolled across the sky.

When dawn came, the willows still rustled in the dying wind, but the great oak lay uprooted and broken in the stream.

Moral: It is better to yield to circumstances beyond your control than to resist them until they destroy you.

THE OLD DOG AND
HIS MASTER

man went hunting one day with his favorite
old hound, a dog who had been his compan-
ion since the man was twelve. Together they
set out to search for the elusive stag of the
deep forest.

They walked for miles through steep-sided river valleys
and across rocky hilltops, looking for some sign of the swift
and secretive animal. At the edge of a high mountain meadow they found him, grazing on the tender new shoots of
early spring grasses.

They quietly circled around until they were quite close
to the stag. Then the hound flung himself across the meadow
and onto the stag's back, biting his neck and digging claws
into his heavily muscled shoulder. The man followed, hoping
to kill the stag with his gun from short range.

The stag dropped its head and twisted its shoulders,
throwing the dog violently to the ground. Then it gored him

with its antlers and kicked him with its front feet. With one glance at the onrushing man, it bounded off across the meadow and disappeared into the dark tree line.

The man ran up to the dog, which lay moaning on the ground. "You useless bag of bones," the man shouted. "Why couldn't you hold on just a little longer? I could have killed that beast."

"How can you criticize me?" growled the hound. "I am old now, and tired because I have spent my life protecting and serving you."

Moral: Selfish fools demand impossible things of those who are closest to them.

THE OLD MAN AND HIS SONS

couple had many sons. The boys were always fighting, but their parents thought they would stop as they grew older. Years passed. The sons continued to argue even after they left home and had their own families.

When their father became old, he worried that his sons would never learn to get along. Over and over he explained to them how important it was to work together, but by the end of his talk his sons would have started to shout at each other.

At last the old man decided to try a new approach. He called his sons together for a meeting. He asked them to gather a bundle of sticks. Then he asked each son to break the bundle.

The oldest went first. Muscles in his forearms bulged and sweat glistened on his brow, but the sticks didn't even crack. The next oldest son laughed at his older brother's failure. He

decided to stand on one end of the bundle and bend the sticks up against his weight. Again, failure. In fact, each son failed miserably.

At last the old man handed one stick from the bundle to each of his sons and asked them to break the sticks. This they did easily, and the entire bundle was quickly broken.

Then the father said, "Oh, my sons, do you see how much power lies in being united? If you would only live in love and friendship, no mortal power could hurt you."

Moral: There is great strength in unity.

The Old Trout, the Young Trout, and the Gudgeon

 fisherman took great pride in tying his own flies. He spent hours collecting just the right materials. Then he patiently assembled his flies, placing each piece of feather and tying each knot with care.

The fisherman also studied how insects behaved on rivers and lakes so that he could imitate them when he cast his line. His artificial flies were so lifelike that most people could not distinguish them from real insects.

One day, he cast his line into a river with so much art that a young trout was certain a juicy insect had landed lightly on the water. She rushed toward it, eager for a snack. Immediately the young trout's mother blocked her path.

"Never rush to act," said the old trout, "when there may be danger. Let someone else take the risk first. You wait. If that's a real insect, it will probably dart away after another

fish attacks it. Then you can be the second one to try. Even if you don't catch it, at least you'll be safe."

Just then, up swam a gudgeon, a small carplike fish. He felt proud that he had beaten the trout to such a delicious insect. He leaped out of the water, snapped at the fly, and swallowed it whole. As he tried to swim away, the gudgeon discovered he was securely hooked. The young trout watched the satisfied fisherman reel in his catch. She understood exactly what might have happened if she herself had rushed ahead.

Moral: Look before you leap.

THE OLD WOMAN
AND HER FAT HEN

n old woman had a beautiful hen. Every morning the hen laid an egg, which the woman ate for breakfast. Sometimes the woman ate cereal for breakfast and used the egg to make warm, berry-filled muffins, chewy cookies, or one-egg chocolate cake.

One day the old woman began thinking about all the things she could make that used more than one egg. To make her famous popovers, she needed two eggs. Rich, cheesy quiche took three eggs. Pound cake called for nine eggs, and angel food cake took a whole dozen. She could save her eggs for several days to make these treats, but she wished she didn't have to wait so long.

It would be very nice to have two eggs a day instead of one, she thought. Surely if I give my hen twice as much barley for her breakfast, she will lay twice as many eggs.

So the old woman began to feed the hen twice as much

grain. At first there was no change, but slowly the hen began to put on weight. One morning the woman went to the barn and discovered the hen hadn't laid any eggs at all. The next day she did lay an egg, so the woman continued to carry out her plan.

Eventually the hen grew so fat that she could hardly waddle around the barnyard. Because of her large size, the hen stopped laying any eggs at all.

Moral: Greedy people push nature beyond its limits and are certain to fail.

THE OLD WOMAN
AND THE WINE JAR

n old woman fell upon hard times. She had
no home and spent each day scavenging for
food scraps and discarded clothes, hoping that
she would find enough to live on. Every
member of her family and every one of her friends were
dead, and she was quite alone in the world.

One day she was going through a pile of smelly garbage
looking for food when she found a clay jar. Holding it to her
nose, she sniffed cautiously at first. The first smile in weeks lit
up her face. "Oh, how delicious," she exclaimed.

The jar had held a fine old wine and still carried the
scent of sweet crushed berries, warm summer evenings, and
joyous times with family and friends. For a moment, the old
woman was transported to an earlier time when all around
her were people who loved her. She felt warmed by each of
their loving hugs, heard again their encouraging words, and
grew stronger because all of them had put their faith in her.

Several times the old woman brought the jar to her nose, breathing deeply of the wine-rich aromas and escaping for the moment into a world of memories she thought that she had lost forever. Tears of joy slipped down her wrinkled cheeks, and she wiped her eyes with gnarled fingers.

In a voice filled with longing, she murmured, "How wonderful must the wine itself have been when it leaves behind such a sweet perfume."

Moral: The memory of a good deed lives on.

The One-Eyed Doe

s she fled from some hunters, a young doe ran past a branch that poked her in the eye. She managed to escape from the hunters, but after a while she could no longer see out of her injured eye. She knew her half blindness would make it harder to evade hunters, so she decided to always graze on a bluff overlooking the sea. That way her blind eye would face the water and her good eye could stay alert for enemies approaching from the forest.

This strategy worked for years, and she felt quite safe. She managed to raise many fawns and she enjoyed life, although she missed being able to graze in the meadows deep in the forest, and she never felt totally comfortable on the woodland paths.

Early one morning, two men were out fishing in a rowboat when one of them pointed east toward a bluff. There stood the doe, her profile in stark relief against the pale grey

sky. Silently the men rowed their boat closer to the bluff. The occasional lap of water folding in around the oars never reached the doe's ears. One of the men raised his rifle, took careful aim, and shot her.

The doe crumpled to the ground. Pain and shock burned through her body. With her dying breath she cried out: "The irony of fate! That I should receive my death wound from the side I thought was safe and be safe on the side where I looked for danger."

Moral: Troubles often come from where we least expect them.

THE OVERFED FOX

fox was hungry, but the day was getting too hot for chasing rabbits and mice. Then he caught the scent of meat. He tilted his head back and sniffed the breeze, trying to determine where the odor was coming from. It seemed to be drifting toward him from the far corner of the meadow. Trotting over, the fox nosed around for the source of the smell. He couldn't see anything, but the smell of meat was stronger, and his stomach rumbled with hunger.

The fox checked the trees along the edge of the meadow. Sure enough, one tree had a hollow where a shepherd had left some bread and meat to eat later in the day. Without a moment's thought, the fox wormed his way through a narrow hole at the top of the hollow and tore into the food. It was quite a feast, and he smacked his lips as he ate.

Once the fox had devoured everything in sight, he tried to squeeze back through the hole. He couldn't get out. All

his gorging had made him too fat to fit through the small space. Turning his nose toward the sky, the fox howled with woe.

Another fox passing by asked what the trouble was. Once the situation was explained, the second fox said, "Patience, my friend. Time cures all misfortunes. You will have to stay there till you become as lean as you were before you climbed in."

Moral: Those who act without thinking things through will often find themselves in unexpected danger.

The Ox and the Frogs

An overgrown ox grazed in a meadow on a late spring day. So intent was he on eating that he did not notice a family of young frogs near the edge of a pond. He lumbered right through their home and stepped on one of the frogs, squashing it into the mud and killing it.

The rest of the frogs clustered around their dead brother. They looked anxiously after the ox as he moved away, the ground shaking under his enormous feet. They feared that the huge beast would return and kill more of them.

When their mother returned from visiting her sister, the young frogs jumped on her, tripping over their words as they hurried to explain the terrible death of their brother. They still trembled with fear when they talked about the great creature who had killed him.

"He's huge," said one. "His foot is bigger than I am. We must find a safer place to live, or he will kill us all."

"A big creature," their mother said. She smiled and puffed herself up. "Was he as big as this?"

"Much bigger, Mother," the young frogs replied.

She puffed herself up even more. "He could not have been bigger than this," she announced.

"Mother," said one of her children, "Don't bother to puff yourself up any more. You would burst before you could get to one-tenth the size of that monster."

Moral: Because of pride, envy, and ambition, people often think of themselves as bigger than they are and underestimate the abilities of others.

The Peacock and
the Crane

peacock spread out his bright tail and turned his head to admire the sun's light reflecting off the iridescent colors. His tail shimmered, and with each movement, its pattern shifted like pieces of colored glass in a kaleidoscope. The peacock was so taken by the sight that he almost hypnotized himself with his own beauty.

Just in time, a long-legged crane walked by and greeted the peacock. "Good day to you, Mr. Peacock," he said politely. "And how are you this fine day?"

"Good day to you, too, good sir," replied the peacock, turning in the sun so that the crane could admire his tail if he cared to. "I could not be feeling better." Then in a voice filled with mock sympathy, he added, "It must be difficult to be a drab and dreary crane. You don't have a bit of color on your wings. Your features are plain, and no one ever comments about your appearance. I, on the other hand, am

robed like a king in gold and purple and all the colors of the rainbow, and people come from miles around to gaze upon my beauty."

"That is true," replied the crane. For a moment, he paused and looked at the peacock's feet. "But we all have our limits," he went on. "I soar to the heights of heaven and lift up my voice to the stars, while you walk below like a rooster and cannot fly away from that manure pile you're standing in."

Moral: Value useful abilities more than beauty.

The Peacock's Complaint to Juno

he powerful goddess Juno thought the peacock was the most beautiful bird on earth. She gave the bird everything he asked for, and much that he hadn't yet thought to ask for. Still the peacock looked sad.

"What's wrong with my favorite bird?" Juno asked. "Don't you have everything you could possibly desire? Why are you so glum? Is there something else I can give you?"

The peacock hung his head. His tail feathers dragged in the dust. "Everyone laughs at my voice," he complained. "But just look at the nightingale. It's a drab bird with no looks to speak of, but it has a beautiful voice that entrances anyone who hears it. This just isn't fair. Why should such a beautiful voice be wasted on such a plain-looking bird? I'll never be happy until I have a fine voice too." The peacock sighed and hung his head even lower.

Much to the peacock's surprise, Juno was not at all sym-

pathetic. Her eyes flashed with anger. "Envious bird," she said in a stern voice, "you have no cause to complain. On your neck shine all the colors of the rainbow, and when you display your tail, it glistens like a mass of priceless gems. No living creature has every good thing. The falcon has swiftness, the eagle, strength, the parrot, speech. You have two gifts—size and beauty. Stop complaining. Remember, it is well within my powers to take back those gifts if you continue to be so ungrateful."

Moral: Be content with your abilities. You can't have everything.

The Pike and
The Dolphin

A handsome pike lived in a river. Other fish swimming past always commented on his size, beauty, and strength. He was the finest fish to be found in the entire river, all the other fish finally agreed, fine enough to be their prince.

The pike, however, was not satisfied with simply being prince of a river. He had heard of something called the sea, an enormous body of water. He planned to expand his kingdom and become ruler of that sea. Confident of his success, he swam down the river to its end, where it emptied into a great stretch of water. This must be the sea, he thought.

The sea was colder than the river where the pike had lived, but he marveled at the huge expanse of water that surrounded him. This, he decided, was a kingdom worthy of his talents and size. Whenever he met a new fish, he announced that he was to be king of the sea.

Word of his claims soon spread throughout the sea, but

some fish objected to his plans. Offended by the pike's arrogance, a large dolphin attacked the would-be king. The pike quickly realized that the dolphin was bigger, faster, and stronger. He had no hope of winning a battle against the dolphin, so he fled back toward his river. The dolphin pursued the pike with such intense anger that only luck brought the pike back safely to his river kingdom.

Relieved to have survived such a fierce attack, the pike decided that ruling his smaller freshwater kingdom would be challenge enough.

Moral: Keep ambition within bounds.

THE PLAYFUL DONKEY

A donkey loved nothing better than to have fun and make people laugh. He was jealous of a monkey who danced, walked on his hands, and turned somersaults, because the monkey drew louder applause and laughter than the donkey ever had.

One day the donkey worked his way up onto the roof of the low building where he had so often seen the monkey perform. The donkey quickly decided that the roof made a better stage than the ground. This explained the monkey's success. People could see him better than they could see the donkey on the ground. He brayed so that people would look up at him, then began to dance. At first only a few people watched his dancing, but the sound of his hooves pounding against the tile roof soon drew a small crowd.

All went well until the donkey's hooves broke some of the tiles. His owner, who until that point hadn't paid any

attention to what his donkey was doing, scrambled up onto the roof in a rage. He quickly drove the donkey off, beating him hard with a thick piece of wood.

The bewildered donkey asked, "Why are you beating me? I saw a monkey do this same dance yesterday, and you laughed so hard you couldn't stand up."

"But the roof is designed to carry the weight of a monkey," said the owner in disgust. "Not the heavy stomping of a foolish donkey like you."

Moral: Those who do not know their place must be taught it.

THE RAVEN AND
THE SWAN

silky black raven lived in a forest along a road where there was plenty of food for him to scavenge. His neighbors respected him, for by feeding on carrion, he helped keep the forest and its creatures healthy. But he was jealous of a swan who flew overhead on her way to and from the lake where she lived. She had brilliant white feathers and a broad wingspan.

"If only I were as beautiful as she," the raven murmured.

He tried to think of a way to make himself as beautiful as the swan. After weeks of discarding one idea after another, he finally figured it out. The swan grew beautiful by drinking the lake's pure water and feeding on its lush green grass instead of eating dead animals the way he did.

Immediately he deserted his home where he had built such a successful life and moved to the shores of the swan's lake. Every waking moment he spent either bathing and preening his feathers or plunging into the cool water to nib-

ble on the fresh-water grasses. The grasses seemed to disagree with his stomach, but the raven ignored this. He was determined to be as beautiful as the swan.

Despite his best efforts, the raven did not grow white like the swan. Worse yet, because he was eating grasses rather than the meat his body was designed to consume, he got thin and sickly. Finally, still no more like the swan than ever, he died.

Moral: Change of scene will not cause a change of nature.

THE REDBREAST AND THE SPARROW

ne October day, a redbreast sat on the branch of an apple tree. She felt the sun warming her feathers, noticed the ripening apples and the bright fall foliage, and opened her mouth to sing. The robin's voice wasn't lyrical or rich, but she didn't mind. She felt good, and she wanted to share her joy with everyone.

Just then her good friend the sparrow landed on the thatched roof of a nearby cottage. "Have you ever compared your thin warblings to the song of the thrush, the blackbird, or the lark?" she asked the robin. "You might notice that other birds listen to such great singing in silence. They are wise enough not to shame the rest of the neighborhood with a feeble imitation of fine music. If I were you, I'd think twice about singing any more. I'm only telling you this for your own good."

"Judge with honesty at least," said the robin, astonished

at her friend's attack. "I respect the great voices you have mentioned, but by no means am I trying to imitate them. Those birds bring joy to everyone by announcing the arrival of spring. That is their role, and I enjoy listening to them as much as the next bird. But now that those songbirds have left for the winter, I'm simply sharing my joy in the best way I know. I only hope that my poor little song will brighten someone's day."

Moral: Rude friends can cause as much hurt as enemies.

FURTHER READINGS

Caduto, Michael J. *Earth Tales from Around the World.* Golden, Colo.: Fulcrum, 1997.

Creedon, Sharon. *Fair is Fair: World Folktales of Justice.* Little Rock, Ark.: August House, 1997.

Czernecki, Stefan. *The Cricket's Cage: A Chinese Folktale.* New York: Hyperion, 1997.

Goble, Paul. *Iktomi and the Buzzard: A Plains Indian Story.* New York: Orchard, 1994.

Gonzalez, Lucia M. *The Bossy Gallito: A Traditional Cuban Folk Tale.* New York: Scholastic, 1994.

Han, Suzanne Crowder. *The Rabbit's Judgment.* New York: Holt, 1994.

London, Jonathan. *What Newt Could Do for Turtle.* Cambridge, Mass.: Candlewick, 1996.

Martin, Rafe, ed. *Mysterious Tales of Japan.* New York: Putnam, 1996.

Mayo, Margaret. *When the World Was Young: Creation and Pourquois Tales.* New York: Simon & Schuster, 1996.

Reneaux, J. J. *Why Alligator Hates Dog: A Cajun Folktale.* Little Rock, Ark.: August House, 1995.

Ross, Gale. *How Turtle's Back Was Cracked: A Traditional Cherokee Tale.* New York: Dial, 1995.

Roth, Susan L. *The Biggest Frog in Australia*. New York: Simon & Schuster, 1996.

Voake, Charlotte. *Ginger.* Cambridge, Mass.: Candlewick, 1997.

Walking Turtle, Eagle. *Full Moon Stories: Thirteen Native American Legends.* New York: Hyperion, 1997.

INDEX ◗

BRUCE and BECKY DUROST FISH are freelance writers and editors who have worked on more than one hundred books for children and young adults. They have degrees in history and literature and live in the high desert of Central Oregon.